A Transformative Time in History

A Teen's Point of View

Arhaan Gupta-Rastogi

A Transformative Time in History
A Teen's Point of View

By Arhaan Gupta-Rastogi

Published by: Nicasio Press, California, USA
ISBN: 979-8-9864100-2-9

Contents

INTRODUCTION

Writing has always been a way for me to express my opinions and use my voice. The first article I ever wrote was about the Green New Deal; ultimately, it revealed a passion that I never knew I had. Throughout middle school, I started to get interested in politics. Coincidentally, it was during Trump's presidency as well. Political problems affected our life, and I was ready to write about them.

The COVID-19 pandemic also occurred, when multiple families passed away and many were afraid to vote for elections. I wrote a number of articles around politics during the pandemic to update those who were not following politics and to provide an opinion for them. I also wrote on the pandemic in general to provide information to readers. Some articles regarding sports were written because all my friends were talking about it and the topic interested me a lot.

Overall, I received a lot of support from friends, family, and others, but there were also some negative comments as I was writing on the "hot" topics at the time. Those comments helped me acknowledge the other side of problems as well as develop a more neutral political view. After every negative comment, I was sure to acknowledge all possible solutions in my articles. I really enjoy writing about political issues and hope to continue in the future.

The proceeds from this book will support two causes that are important to me: The Ronald McDonald House and National Digital Inclusion Alliance.

The Ronald McDonald House supports children while they are sick and undergoing treatment. Even as a young child, I would ask my friends to donate to them instead of bringing me gifts. Over the years I have taken my books and games for the children to use during their stay. Half of the proceeds from this book will continue to help these children during their time of need.

National Digital Inclusion Alliance combines grassroots community engagement with technical knowledge, research, and policy to advocate for digital equity. I believe strongly that technology can solve problems and therefore, it is important that everyone has access. The other half of the proceeds from this book will be contributed directly to this cause so we can decrease the digital divide.

POLITICS

Get The Vote Out!

Every four years, we can count on one thing: presidential elections. When they are a few days away, it's the time to ask: Have the adults in your life voted? Are the adults in your life planning to vote? If not, you might ask them if they've enjoyed the last three years, and if they're better off now than they were in the previous administration. Either way, they need to vote. Voting is the right of every U.S. citizen over the age of eighteen, and our democracy cannot work if we don't vote. Our votes dictate the policies that shape our lives and our future: everything from school funding to social security.

If you're a kid like me, then you can't vote yet. This is a bummer, but it doesn't mean that you can't influence others. An average of only 55% of eligible people vote in U.S. presidential elections (as of 2016), and that's not nearly high enough to keep our republic healthy and moving forward. In fact, the U.S. places 26th in voter turnout among OECD countries. This means that 25 developed countries (including Canada and Mexico) have higher voter turnout rates than we do. We can do better!

It's time for us to get adults out to vote. We're already good at convincing them—how many of us have smartphones or spend way too much time playing video games? The truth is, we have a lot of influence over our elders. They'll listen to us, in part because deep down they know what's right. Women only got the right to vote in the U.S. in 1920, and they had to sacrifice a lot for that. African-Americans have struggled to vote for over a century, and we can't just dismiss their sacrifices. The next time adults complain about the hassle of filling out a ballot and turning it in, remind them of life in the South before the 1965 Voting Rights Act.

There are many ways to vote in California. You can mail in a ballot, or drop a ballot off at a designated dropbox; you can go to your county elections office and fill out your ballot and submit early; and you can vote in-person on election day. Voting early is the best bet, as then you know your vote will be counted. Say what you want about California Secretary of State Alex Padilla, but he definitely made it easy to vote. With all these ways to cast a ballot, it's easier than ever to make our voices heard. We just need to make sure that the adults around us carry out their minimal civic duties.

In the end, even though we kids can't vote, we can still do our part. This means getting our parents and other adults out there to vote. If they're worried about any health issues running rampant, (which makes sense), then they can mail in their ballot or drop it off at a designated dropbox. Easy! So let's beat Canada and Mexico this time, and really get out the vote. Our future always depends on it.

An Inauguration Like No Other

My mom made me watch the presidential inauguration ceremony when it happened in January, 2020. I didn't exactly put up resistance, but watching a political ceremony also wasn't my first choice of things to do. In the end, I was happy that Joe Biden and Kamala Harris were sworn in, and there were three moments that stood out for me. In the first place, it was weird to watch Joe and Jill Biden walk alone into the White House without being greeted by the outgoing president and first lady. It was also cool to watch Justice Sotomayor give the oath of office to Harris. Finally, I was struck by Amanda Gorman's inaugural poem. Between Justice Sotamayor, Kamala Harris, and Amanda Gorman, I thought that there were a lot of "firsts" at that inauguration.

I remember in 2016 how Barack and Michelle Obama welcomed Donald and Melania Trump to the White House. Nobody thought that the Obamas were happy to do this, or that they were in any way happy to spend time with the Trumps. But they did it, mostly because it's what outgoing presidents do to help ensure a peaceful transition. To watch the Bidens enter the White House without the Trumps there to greet them was strange. I wish it were the only strange thing to have occurred since the election, but that was not our country at the time.

It was an incredible moment when Senator Amy Klobuchar introduced Supreme Court Justice Sonia Sotamayor. She introduced Sotomayor as the first Latinx justice to give the vice-presidential oath of office to the first woman, African American, and South Asian American to serve as vice-president. In a way, these were two memorable moments brought together in one important juncture. Harris's election means a lot to me personally, as it gives me concrete proof that Indian Americans can occupy positions of political leadership in the United States. I may never run for higher office, but she makes it clear that it is at least possible.

Perhaps the most dramatic moment of the inauguration was Amanda Gorman's reading of "The Hill We Climb," a poem she had written. When I was listening to the poem, I couldn't quite understand what her point was. However, the way it was presented was good. Although it might not have had the best rhyme to it, it still presented its point, and I understood why it was in the inauguration. One line that stuck with me was "It's the past we step into and how we repair it," because of how it brings attention to moving forward and how that will bring a bright future to all.

Election for CA-District 14

In 2022, California's District 14 representative Jackie Speier announced her retirement. Speier had held this position for nine years, and her retirement opened up a race for her open seat. District 14 covers much of the region just north of SHP up to San Francisco including Redwood City, San Mateo, Belmont, and all the way out to Pacifica. This is the home of many gators, and the candidate who wins will represent the voice of a great portion of our community. In the polls, Democrat Eric Swalwell led the polls running against republican Alison Hayden.

Representative Swalwell, who currently represents California's 15th congressional district, covering much of the East Bay, passed the primary and was on the ballot on November 8, 2022. He has represented District 15 since 2013; however in 2022, he ran in the 14th congressional district. Swalwell was also a presidential candidate in the 2020 election, although his campaign, which focused on gun control, was unsuccessful.

He focuses on developing policies that support equality, opportunity, and security. During his time as the U.S. House representative for District 15, he served on multiple sub-committees in the house, such as the House Permanent Select Committee on Intelligence and the Intelligence Modernization and Readiness Subcommittee, which both work to oversee intelligence agencies in the U.S. and ensure they have the resources they need to function. He strongly feels that protecting citizens is the government's most solemn duty and believes that resources should be spent on personnel management, security clearance reform, information technology modernization, and other areas. He also serves on the House Judiciary Committee, where he works on improving justice reforms and addresses voting rights, LGBTQ equality, protecting women's rights, and health care.

Swalwell's opponent, Alison Hayden, has a very different background. She was raised in an Air Force family, grew up in Taiwan, and has a lot of experience with the military. She also has a long history in finance and banking, having spent eight years working with different banks and private investors. She also served in the U.S. Peace Corps within its Business Development Group, has brought power to the National Alternative Women's Association, and launched projects related to teaching ethics and business.

She has spent a lot of time working on education, which appeals to a big part of her political base. She worked with felons to help them earn their high school GEDs, and also earned teaching credentials in secondary and special education, working with schools all around San Francisco. She also volunteered her time to work with those who are recovering from alcohol and drug addiction. She is a strong believer in stopping inflation through the Glass-Steagall Act, finishing building the wall, increasing security to ensure families are protected, giving schools better opportunities to learn, and providing better healthcare to those in her area in any way she can.

Swalwell led the polls with around 63 percent of the votes. If the election had ended before November, all cities within District 14 could be looking at a more revolutionized future with more tech, more LGBTQ rights, and more women's rights. If Hayden were to make a comeback and win the election, we could be looking at an increase in security, an attempt at improving the public schools education, better healthcare for those in need, and a very family forward platform supporting the pro-life movement. SHP students, faculty, and staff who live in this district will be affected because the policies passed by whoever holds this seat, will apply to you. The election is coming up fast, and everyone has to be ready to vote!

Sources
https://swalwell.house.gov/about/full-biography
https://alison4congress.com/meet-alison

ERA Past and Present

March is women's history month, so it's a good time to focus on the importance of equal rights. In January 2022, Congress put forth a bipartisan resolution to extend the deadline to ratify the Equal Rights Amendment (ERA), which was introduced in 1972. Most young people have never heard of the ERA, so it's worth describing its main points, why some Americans have opposed it, and where things stand now.

The ERA proposes to make illegal any federal or state law that discriminates on the basis of sex. This means that women must be paid as much as men, and they must generally have the same rights and protections as men. This is largely an economic issue, since even today women make on average 77 cents for every dollar earned by a man. Even the U.S. tax code is written to privilege men and make women economically dependent on their male spouses. In the early 1970s, the women's movement and their allies sought to do away with these injustices through a constitutional amendment.

While there was broad bipartisan support for the ERA, conservative Christian groups were mostly opposed to it. One woman in particular, Phyllis Schlafly, argued that the ERA undermined traditional values and benefits afforded women. She argued that the ERA would force women to serve in combat during wars and that alimony laws that supported divorced women would disappear. She would often begin her speeches by thanking her husband for allowing her to leave the house, a nod to her traditional, Christian values.

As the opposition movement gained steam, the ratification process for the ERA began to stall. Thirty-five states ratified the ERA in the 1970s, but then things began to unravel. Five states—Idaho, South Dakota, Nebraska, Kentucky, and Tennessee—ratified the ERA but then rescinded their ratification. The congressional deadline to ratify the ERA passed in 1982, and at that time, only thirty states (if one accepts Idaho, South Dakota, Nebraska, Kentucky, and Tennessee's right to rescind) have ratified the ERA.

Over the past five years, Nevada, Illinois, and Virginia voted to ratify the ERA. If we deny the right of Idaho, South Dakota, Nebraska, Kentucky, and Tennessee to rescind their ratification, and we allow Nevada, Illinois, and Virginia to ratify the ERA after the deadline, then the ERA is set for passage. As with most things in the U.S., the courts will ultimately decide. In a DC federal court on March 7, 2021, a judge ruled that Nevada's, Illinois's, and Virginia's ratifications were not valid. Congress has the legal power to remove its deadline retroactively, but this would have to be passed in the House and the Senate. It will likely pass in the House, but it's doubtful that it will pass in the Senate, where conservative senators see the ERA as a direct threat to anti-abortion legislation in their home states.

All of this signals an uphill battle for equal rights in the U.S. The U.S. Senate remains an issue (where small rural states like Wyoming have just as much representation as California, and the filibuster requires most bills to pass by a two-thirds majority), and it's doubtful that the courts will side with ERA proponents. All that is needed is a retroactive extension of the deadline and an exclusion of five states' decision to revoke their previous ratification.

This is a tall order, and even the late Ruth Bader Ginsburg felt that it may be best simply to start over with a fresh amendment. True equal rights for women remains a viable goal, but it won't happen without a lot of work and sacrifice.

Impeachment: Round II

In the history of the United States, exactly one presidential candidate has lost and refused to concede. That same candidate, Donald Trump, is also the only sitting president to have been impeached twice in the House of Representatives. Many on the political right questioned whether it made any sense to impeach Trump a second time, but it was the correct move. First, Trump incited the violent insurrection on January 6, 2020 that led to five deaths, and it is also likely that his team helped coordinate it. For these two crimes, there must be accountability. The other benefit to the second impeachment is that it can prevent Trump from ever holding federal office in the future.

Trump's words near the end of his speech on January 6, 2020, are perhaps the most incriminating. After listing his achievements as president and calling President-Elect Biden an "illegitimate president," he said the following:

"And we fight. We fight like hell. And if you don't fight like hell, you're not going to have a country anymore. Our exciting adventures and boldest endeavors have not yet begun. My fellow Americans, for our movement, for our children, and for our beloved country. And I say this despite all that's happened. The best is yet to come. So we're going to, we're going to walk down Pennsylvania Avenue."

It is worth mentioning that Trump is saying all of this from behind bulletproof glass, a rare sight at his rallies. Why was it there? It was there almost certainly because the Secret Service knew that there would be thousands of armed people at the rally. So here Trump was exhorting thousands of his armed supporters to march to the Capitol and "fight like hell" for their country.

Beyond Trump's incendiary remarks on January 6, there is also evidence that the violent insurrection that followed was carefully coordinated by people working with the president. One key piece of evidence is a letter sent to the head of the DC National Guard by acting Secretary of Defense Christopher C. Miller on January 4. Maj. Gen. William J. Walker had requested that he be permitted to mobilize the DC National Guard after receiving credible reports that the January 6 rally was likely to turn violent.[1] In Miller's reply, he makes it clear that the DC National Guard did not have permission to engage in any sort of meaningful crowd control. They could not wear helmets or body armor, they could not make arrests, and they could not coordinate with law enforcement or other National Guard units (@lukebroadwater). How is one to read this letter? Why would Trump's recently appointed acting Defense Secretary put such limits on the activities of DC's National Guard? President Trump ended his January 6 rally speech at 1:10 p.m., and by 2:20 p.m., the rioters had breached the Capitol and were moving freely through its chambers and halls. It was only at 3:04 p.m. that Miller finally gave permission to mobilize the DC National Guard. Since it took time for members of the DCNG to arrive at their posts, the first group did not

---

[1] 28 Jan. 2021, 9:00 AM, twitter.com/lukebroadwater/status/ 1354836817925832705. "Here's the Jan. 4 memo from former acting Defense Secretary requiring "personal authorization" for DC National Guard to employ riot control agents & other tactics at Jan. 6 "March for Trump." This same day Capitol police knew of a "strong potential" for violence against Congress."

arrive at the Capitol until 5:40 p.m. Perhaps Miller was simply inept (a possibility), but his January 4 letter and January 6 delay in calling up the DCNG certainly make it look as though he was aiding and abetting the rioters.

The benefit of the impeachment trial is that the American people could know the extent of the plot to overturn the 2020 presidential election. Who was involved and to what extent? Without an investigation and accountability, we never would have known. And if we never know, then it is highly likely that such an insurrection could occur again. We needed to determine who was culpable for the crimes of January 6, and since the president himself seems to have triggered it, the process clearly involved him. Whatever the extent of Trump's guilt, the other benefit of this second impeachment is that we might be able to ensure that he is never eligible to hold federal office again.

The Republicans are right that no president has ever been impeached after leaving office, and they're also right that Trump's second impeachment is legally unprecedented. This does not mean that it is unconstitutional, and it also does not mean that it was a bad idea. If we are ever to restore democratic normalcy to our country, we must find the people behind the January 6 coup attempt (let's call it what it was) and bring them to justice. This includes the former president, and to get there, we need a trial. In the end, the second impeachment is about turning the page on the past four years and building a foundation for moving forward.

Joe Biden and Powdered Creamer

On an episode of HBO's "Real Time," host Bill Maher famously compared Joe Biden to powdered coffee creamer. "Nobody loves it," Maher explained, "but in a jam, it gets the job done." I understand what Maher means here, but I also think it's a little unfair. Biden is more than just an upgrade from Donald Trump. His presidency will almost certainly bring with it greater access to healthcare, more progressive tax policies, and a serious plan to fight climate change. These are three serious issues, and even if Biden makes progress in these areas, he's much more than just "okay in a jam."

On healthcare, Biden plans to strengthen the Affordable Care Act, which a majority of Americans claim to support.[2] He hopes to add a public option to ACA, which was originally part of the 2010 proposal before Sen. Joe Lieberman (D-CT) had it removed.[3] This would allow people to buy their health insurance from the federal government at a reduced rate. Biden also wants to expand ACA's tax credits to poor people so that their premiums will be even lower. So far, he hasn't expressed support for Medicare for All, but that is certainly the direction things are heading.

---

[2] Hamel, Liz. "5 Charts About Public Opinion on the Affordable Care Act and the Supreme Court." Kaiser Family Foundation, 16 Oct. 2020, www.kff.org/health-reform/poll- finding/5-charts-about-public-opinion-on-the-affordable-care-act-and-the-supreme-court/.

[3] Norman, Jane, and John Reichard. "Senate Democrats Drop the Public Option to Woo Lieberman, and Liberals Howl." The Commonwealth Fund, 15 Dec. 2009, commonwealthfund.org /publications/newsletter-article/ senate-democrats-drop-public-option-woo-lieberman-and-liberals-howl.

In terms of tax policy, Biden plans to increase taxes on the wealthy while decreasing the tax burden of low-income earners. This is a progressive tax plan, meaning that the wealthy pay more (as a share of income) than the poor. Biden plans to "raise taxes on individuals with income above $400,000,[4]" and this includes raising individual income tax, capital gains tax, and payroll taxes. He would also raise the corporate income tax rate to 28%. This will generate income for the U.S. Treasury and ease the tax burden of most Americans. This is sorely needed after all the money the federal government spent trying to prevent a Coronavirus depression and the desperate shape many American families are in as a result of the pandemic. Biden has also said that he wishes to forgive all student-loan debt, which would allow lower-income and middle-class Americans to write off over $1.6 trillion in debt, a move that will likely stimulate spending.

Biden's climate plan would push the U.S. economy to 100% clean energy and net-zero emissions by 2050. Much of this goal depends on the passage of some version of the Green New Deal, and Biden seems to be supportive of that. He also favors investment in clean-energy infrastructure designed to meet climate goals and create new jobs. As a president with enormous foreign-policy experience, he also plans to use the office of the president to encourage other nations to get on board with clean-energy investment. As a longtime train commuter, it's also reasonable to assume that Biden will invest fully in public transportation.

---

[4] Watson, Garrett, Huaqun Li, and Taylor LaJoie. "Details and Analysis of President-elect Joe Biden's Tax Plan." Tax Foundation, 22 Oct. 2020, taxfoundation.org/joe-biden-tax- plan-2020

In the end, Joe Biden has integrated many of his previously ambitious policies into his presidency. He has made significant changes to health care, federal tax policy, and our national response to climate change. Biden isn't just an "okay-in-a-jam" president; he promises to be a pretty good president. He has experience in the Senate and the White House, which has come in hand as he approaches the midway point of his presidency.

.

On the Passing of Ruth Bader Ginsburg

The passing of Ruth Bader Ginsburg on September 18, 2020, was a tragedy for our country. This is perhaps a strange thing to say about someone who lived to be 87, but when it comes to Supreme Court justices, timing matters. It's true that the U.S. lost a powerful voice for equal rights with RBG's death, but when Donald Trump nominated his third Supreme Court justice, the makeup of our highest court took a huge step to the right. And given that he's nominated People of Praise member and federal judge Amy Coney Barrett to the bench, things could and did get strange very quickly. Perhaps most tragically, Coney Barrett's appointment makes it entirely possible that RBG's lifetime of work for women's rights will be undone.

What were RBG's main accomplishments? Besides graduating at the top of her class at Columbia Law School, she also fought for equal rights as a law professor. While at Rutgers Law School, Ginsburg discovered that male professors at the University all had higher salaries than their female counterparts. She and other women at the University filed a successful Equal Pay Act complaint. At Columbia Law School, she successfully fought so that her female colleagues could earn the same retirement benefits as the men. She also co-founded the ACLU's Women's Rights Project, winning five cases that she argued before the Supreme Court. Ginsburg also fought hard for the LGBTQ community, undocumented immigrants, and disabled people. She also worked to expand and protect voting rights for all Americans.

Who is Amy Coney Barrett, Trump's pick to replace RBG on the Supreme Court? She's a 7th Circuit Federal

Appeals Court judge, and a staunch conservative. A devout Catholic, she has already argued against Roe v. Wade, and she is also on record opposing the Affordable Care Act. She even criticized Chief Justice Roberts's recent decision to uphold the ACA. Since a challenge to the ACA is already on the Supreme Court's schedule, its protections have been limited, but they still exist. This is especially bad, since the ACA prevents insurance companies from denying claims due to pre-existing conditions, and over seven million Americans now have Covid-19 as a pre-existing condition. RBG was a staunch supporter of maximizing health care access, and she was also a reliable vote for maintaining Roe v. Wade. With Coney Barrett on the Supreme Court, things changed dramatically. This is likely a dream for the Republicans, but it is a tragedy for RBG's legacy.

With a new 6-3 conservative majority on the Supreme Court, much of RBG's work over the past several decades has been erased. Imagine spending your adult life fighting to secure women's rights and then having it all undone only months after your death. To add insult to injury, Trump nominated Coney Barrett to the Supreme Court on September 26, a full three days before RBG's funeral. Coney Barrett is, like Antonin Scalia before her, the very antithesis of RBG. Why did RBG not retire under Obama? There are two reasons for this. First, there was no guarantee that the Republicans in the Senate would ever even vote on an Obama nominee. Second, she made it clear that she felt sure that Hillary Clinton would be elected, and she was anxious to see her replacement nominated by the country's first woman president. To say that things worked out differently is an understatement.

In the end, RBG's legal successes on the Supreme Court will almost certainly be undone by Coney Barrett in a matter of months. This is much like what Trump did to eight years of Obama's achievements. RBG was a champion for equal rights, and she cared for the country as if we were all her family. She tried to hold on until the election, but her body prohibited her from doing this. Since RBG's death, the future of our country has been murky.

The Darn Electoral College

How is it that a presidential candidate can win by over four million votes, and yet the race can be still "too close to call?" Blame it on the electoral college, the unique and increasingly inconvenient way we select our presidents. Why did the framers of the U.S. Constitution feel the electoral college was necessary? What are its benefits? How is it that candidates for president can lose the popular vote and still win? And is it right that we have to spend several days waiting for volunteers in Pima County, AZ, and Allegheny County, PA, to count every last mail-in ballot?

First, a little history. In 1787, the framers of the U.S. Constitution recognized they needed an executive to make certain necessary decisions, but they weren't sure about how to select one. A direct popular vote frightened many of the framers because they feared that a populist might manipulate voters and skew the election. Their plan was that Congress should appoint the president. Other framers disliked this idea, since they felt it would invite corruption and backroom deals. This impasse lasted for months, but they finally reached a compromise. According to this compromise, each state would select a number of electors based on population. These electors would then vote for the president. The idea was to avoid direct popular election while also taking the process out of the hands of Congress. None of the framers seemed to be thrilled with this compromise, but after months of arguing, they were ready to move on to other issues.

The first crisis of the electoral college had to do with what is often referred to as the "three-fifths compromise." Southern states wanted the electoral college to consider enslaved Black people to be part of their population, even though they denied these people the legal rights of citizens. Northern states argued that it was unacceptable to classify people as "property" but then ask to re-classify them as "residents" for purposes of the electoral college. To many framers, this was merely a cynical power grab on the part of Southern states, since the greater the population of a state the larger its number of electors. In the end (big surprise), they came up with a compromise: each enslaved Black person in a Southern state would count as three-fifths of a person for the purpose of designating electors. So then, if South Carolina had a total population of 250,000 people in 1789, and 43% of its population consisted of enslaved people, then there were 142,500 free residents in South Carolina and 107,500 enslaved people. Since each enslaved person counted as three-fifths of a person, the enslaved population counted as 64,500 people for the purpose of assigning electors to the electoral college. This brought South Carolina to a total electoral population of 207,000 people and gave it seven electoral votes. In 1868, the Fourteenth Amendment repealed the three-fifths compromise, but the electoral college remained.

What are the benefits of the electoral college? First of all, if you live in a mostly rural state such as Iowa or Pennsylvania, the electoral college forces candidates to spend time campaigning in your state. If we elected presidents by national popular vote, would they spend so much time in rural Ohio and Georgia, or would they campaign in large metro areas like New York City and Los Angeles? They'd probably go where the most votes are to be found, and rural states would be neglected. The other major issue is that a popular national vote might end with a winner who got less than 50% of the vote. If we imagine an election with a strong third-party candidate, it doesn't seem too far-fetched that the winner might receive less than 50% of the vote. Would we feel okay electing a president who received the support of less than half the country? With all its problems, the electoral college at least spares us this one.

The electoral college is not without its benefits, but now that five candidates have won the presidency while losing the popular vote (and two in just the past twenty years), it may be time to revisit the value of the electoral college. We may end up with presidents who earn less than 50% of the vote, but this seems better than electing presidents who lose the popular vote by 500,000 votes (George W. Bush in 2000) and three million votes (Donald Trump in 2016). It also would save us from having to care so much about the wishes of people who live in "swing states" with relatively low populations. Who knows? Maybe Pennsylvania is also sick of being bombarded by political ads every four years.

The Debates

The debates for the 2020 presidential election were a mess. The vice-presidential debate between Kamala Harris and Mike Pence was more civil than the presidential debates, but they were still tough to watch. The stars of the vice-presidential debate turned out to be the housefly on Pence's head and Harris's withering smile at all of Pence's interruptions. The presidential debate had no star, and with all its interruptions and name-calling, it turned out to be embarrassing. Beyond all this, both debates were filled with lies and distortions, mostly from the Republican candidates.

The most obvious thing about the vice-presidential debate is that a debate actually took place. There were statements, rebuttals, and a moderator mostly keeping things under control. Even so, Pence had a tendency to interrupt Harris and take away some of her speaking time. Harris was clearly playing it safe (her side had a large lead in the polls), and Pence seemed to have trouble making any sort of positive argument about the Trump administration's record. Even the fact that the two candidates were separated by plexiglass made it pretty clear that Pence, the head of the White House's Covid-19 task force, had done a poor job. And then a fly landed on Pence's head and wouldn't leave for two full minutes. It was distracting, but it was also entertaining. That fly wound up with over 100 Twitter accounts in its name. When this is the high point of a debate, you know things are going poorly.

Where to begin with the presidential debate? CNN's Jake Tapper referred to it as a "hot mess in a dumpster fire in a train wreck," and he probably didn't go far enough. It was bad. Biden had to fight just to get a word in, and Trump persistently broke the rules of the debate. At one point, Biden asked Trump, "Will you shut up, man?" To be clear, this is a former vice-president speaking to a sitting president in the context of an election campaign. It's really sad. There was supposed to be a second debate, but then Trump caught Covid-19 and refused to participate in a virtual debate with Biden. This move backfired because Trump accepted a town hall format and spent over twenty minutes being grilled by Savannah Guthrie.

One particularly troubling exchange involved Trump's retweet of a debunked conspiracy theory about Biden ordering Navy Seals to be murdered to cover up the faked death of Osama Bin Laden. When Guthrie pushed Trump, he said, "That was a retweet, that was an opinion of somebody, and that was a retweet. I'll put it out there, people can decide for themselves, I don't take a position." "I don't get that," Guthrie responded. "You're the president—you're not like someone's crazy uncle who can just retweet whatever!" At the Biden town hall, things were more calm, as Biden laid out his plans for the next four years. He fudged some answers and dodged others, but it was pretty ordinary. Complaining about the tone of the Biden event, Trump adviser Mercedes Schlapp wrote, "Well @JoeBiden @ABCPolitics town hall feels like I am watching an episode of Mister Rodgers [sic] Neighborhood." The point here is that Schlapp felt that Biden was getting easy treatment while Trump was getting grilled. This might be true, but then Biden wasn't responsible for 218,000 American deaths from Covid-19, the worst economic collapse since 1929, and a steep rise in racial violence.

It's reasonable to argue that presidential debates are not really that important. I agree with this, but I also think it's good to have candidates present their ideas with people there to fire back at them. The 2020 debates were something else, however, and I'm not sure that we'll ever have presidential debates again in the future. You can add this to the long list of public things that Trump has broken.

Point of View

CLIMATE CHANGE AND GLOBAL AFFAIRS

Climate Change and California

Living in the Bay Area, it used to be easy to ignore all the talk about climate change. Then the wildfires came, turned our skies Halloween orange, and made it unhealthy to go outside. The pandemic had already made it risky to see our friends and family, but now it was potentially deadly even to go for a walk. This brought climate change home for many of us, and now there's no excuse not to take the problem seriously. Since there may still be doubters out there, it's worth asking: how exactly does climate change impact California? Right now, there are three main areas of concern: wildfires, drought, and sea-level rise.

It's true that wildfires have always been a part of California's ecosystem. It's also true that fire suppression policies since 1905 have left too much of our forests ripe for fire. This isn't the whole story, though. With the higher temperatures brought by climate change, California's fire season is now longer and more severe than ever. According to Cal Fire's website, "warmer spring and summer temperatures, reduced snowpack, and earlier spring snowmelt create longer and more intense dry seasons that increase moisture stress on vegetation and make forests more susceptible to severe wildfire."[5] These changes have also led to an expansion in the size of our fires. Since the early 1970s, wildfires in California have

---

5 "2020 Incident Archive." Cal Fire, www.fire.ca.gov/incidents/2020/, accessed on 18 Sept. 2020.

increased in size by 800 percent.[6] In the year 2020 alone, 3,472,947 acres of our state burned. That's about 2.6 million football fields, or three percent of the whole state. If we don't act now to reduce CO^2 and methane emissions, we may run out of land to burn.

Drought is another perennial issue in California, but it's gotten much worse over the past forty years. According to a 2015 report in the *New York Times*, "rising temperatures dry the soil faster and cause more rapid evaporation from streams and reservoirs."[7] This problem might be manageable if we could expect more rain, but this isn't in the cards. According to the EPA, "precipitation is unlikely to increase as much as evaporation."[8] This will lead to drier soil and a greater need for irrigation water. Unfortunately, "higher temperatures and declining rainfall in nearby states have reduced the flow of water in the Colorado River, a key source of irrigation water in southern California," which is now caught in a dryness loop that will only get more severe with time.

Climate change will also bring rising sea levels, which will flood many parts of the Bay Area. According to *The*

---

[6] Meyer, Robinson. "California's Wildfires Are 500 Percent Larger Due to Climate Change." The Atlantic, 16 Jul. 2019, www.theatlantic.com/science/archive/2019/07/climate- change-500-percent-increase-california-wildfires/594016/

[7] Gillis, Justin. "California Drought Is Made Worse by Global Warming, Scientists Say." New York Times, 20 Aug. 2015, www.nytimes.com/2015/08/21/science/climate-change-intensifies-california-drought-scientists-say.html

[8] "What Climate Change Means for California." Environmental Protection Agency, Aug. 2016, www.epa.gov/sites/production/files/2016-09/documents/climate-change-ca.pdf

ART Bay Shoreline Flood Explorer, which maps the effects of a serious rainstorm, after a four-foot rise in sea levels cities like Alameda, Redwood Shores, Foster City, and East Palo Alto will be completely underwater.[9] Both SFO and Oakland Airport will similarly be flooded. According to the EPA, homes along some ocean shores "will fall into the water as beaches, bluffs, and cliffs erode."[10] The sea will also flood San Francisco Bay wetlands and other estuaries, and this would have a devastating effect on fish and birds in the region.

In the end, climate change has already begun to have a devastating effect on California, and particularly on the Bay Area. Between the wildfires, droughts, and rising sea levels, most of California is in for a bumpy ride.

What can we do? One proposed response is the Green New Deal, a "massive program of investments in clean-energy jobs and infrastructure, meant to transform not just the energy sector, but the entire economy. It is meant both to decarbonize the economy and to make it fairer and more just."[11] It remains to be seen if this plan will go through, or if some revised package sees the light of day. Whatever happens, there's no time to lose.

---

[9] Graff, Amy. "Map in New Study Shows Impact of 4-Foot Sea-Level Rise on San Francisco Bay Area." SF Gate, 17 Dec. 2019, www.sfgate.com/bayarea/article/Sea-level-rise-map- San-Francisco-Bay-Area-14913722.php#photo-1877527

[10] What Climate Change Means for California." Environmental Protection Agency, Aug. 2016, www.epa.gov/sites/production/files/ 2016-09/documents/climate-change-ca.pdf

[11] Roberts, David. "The Green New Deal, Explained." Vox, 30 Mar. 2019, www.vox.com/energy- and-environment/ 2018/12/21/18144138/green-new-deal-alexandria-ocasio-cortez

We Need The Green New Deal

Our world will become a much more hazardous place unless we stop climate change. The United States contributes to climate change by producing carbon dioxide and other greenhouse gasses that heat up our atmosphere. The Green New Deal (GND) is a plan to stimulate the U.S. economy while transitioning the country to 100% renewable, zero-emission energy sources by 2045. If the GND passes, it will make a significant positive impact on our country. There are three reasons for this. They are: the effects of climate change are serious and require immediate action, the creation of many new jobs for the working class, and the government investment that accompanies the plan will spark a new era of technological innovation.

First, the effects of climate change are serious and potentially disastrous. The recent polar vortex storm in the Midwest in 2020 is evidence of this. At the time of the storm, then-President Trump tweeted, "In the beautiful Midwest, wind-chill temperatures are reaching minus 60 degrees, the coldest ever recorded. In coming days, expected to get even colder. People can't last outside even for minutes. What the hell is going on with Global Warming? Please come back fast, we need you!" The former president is confusing weather with climate. Though they are closely related; one is short term and one is long-term weather predictions. In fact, large fluctuations in temperature are a symptom of climate change.

Temperature differences from normal around the globe for the planet averaged over the past five years (2014-2018). Data from NASA shows that extreme temperatures have become the new normal across the globe.

To address the extremes, we need to diminish our emission of greenhouse gasses by a significant amount within the next five years. If we wait, the damage may be impossible to reverse. As Dr. Schmidt, NASA Climatologist, has said, "We're no longer talking about a situation where global warming is something in the future." The GND is an ambitious plan to reduce greenhouse gas emission and head off the worst damage caused by climate change. In conclusion, the GND can only help us, it cannot hurt us.

Second, the GND also promises to create new jobs for average Americans. Like the New Deal of the 1930s, it is a series of federal programs aimed at stimulating economic growth and creating jobs. There are currently very few manufacturing jobs left in the U.S., and most of these jobs may not come back. This has had a devastating effect on communities and families throughout the country. The GND will invest heavily in manufacturing solar panels, wind turbines, electric vehicles, and others sorts of technologies. This will create new manufacturing jobs for many Americans and strengthen our economy. In conclusion, the idea is that we can save the planet and provide jobs.

Finally, in the 1960s, the federal government invested heavily in space exploration. Without NASA and all the engineers it employed, would we have reached the moon? Would we have all the new technologies that have emerged from our space program? The GND offers a similar opportunity for the U.S. to take the lead in scientific innovation. As a young person, I'm excited to think of what new technologies might appear through a plan to stop climate change and transform our world. I'm even more excited to be a part of this innovation someday.

All in all, climate change is a dangerous thing for our world, and it needs to be stopped before it is too late. Stopping climate change does not have to mean eliminating growth and giving up jobs for working families. The GND has not passed yet, but it is one of the most important initiatives of our time. It should pass. As a young person whose future depends on the survival of the planet, I see the GND as a key to our survival and an important tool for helping the whole world to thrive.

Tropical Storm Eta

Florida has had many chaotic storms throughout the years. One storm that was exceptionally big in 2020 was called Eta. Tropical storms have high winds and extremely hard rainfall. Some issues with tropical storms are that they often cause deaths, they destroy houses, and they can damage local passages.

Death will occasionally be involved with the impact of a tropical storm. For example, researchers stated, "The tropical storm Allison left the people of Texas devastated after 27 casualties." The tropical storm Eta headed for Florida and based on the news, this storm was easily predicted to be a pretty bad and severe storm. The impacts of tropical storms can be extremely severe. The impact of tropical storm Eta resulted in less dramatic effects than hurricane Ian. Flooding is often what will cause people to die. They will be stuck under debris from the destruction of their house, then the water levels will rise because of the intense rain. They will drown and slowly die.

Housing is destroyed in almost every tropical storm. Housing is occasionally what will harm someone. When tropical storms hit land, they can generate 150 mph winds, and their ferocious winds can knock a building down easily. *Newsweek* exclaimed in 2020, "Homes destroyed weeks ago by Hurricane Laura... Laura had a maximum wind speed of 150 mph." This explains the impacts of Hurricane Laura and the impacts a tropical storm can have on housing. This hurricane ended up knocking down between 39 to 45 houses and almost killing several people, leaving many injured. Houses are not easy to repair and certainly aren't cheap. Tropical storms have a massive impact not just on the house itself, but also on the person who owns the house. Some might be scared and frightened by these catastrophic events. Tropical storm Eta was very dangerous and knocked many houses down when it hit Florida.

Floods and other aftereffects of tropical storms can do bad things to roads, bridges, railroads, and other transportation passages. Often, it will pick apart the roads making them unstable, or it will break a bridge not letting you pass it. These impacts can affect every working person's daily life. For example, my cousin has to travel across the Golden Gate Bridge every day to get to work. If our bridge were to break down, then he couldn't go to work. Then other problems will occur through a ripple effect. On streets many weird things have been spotted because of floods—wildlife from the ocean have been spotted on the streets because that's how high and severe the floods were.

The *Orlando Sentinel* addressed this: "Shark was spotted swimming on the highway after Hurricane Harvey." This shows that floods can be so big and can damage your highway by breaking the borders so that sharks could get in. If sharks could get in, then the water levels must have been high, and buildings and passages were destroyed in order for a shark to get into the highway.

The roads were also damaged by tropical storm Eta. When the roads get damaged it takes time and is difficult to repair them, which will affect some people's daily lives.

In the end, tropical storm Eta was a very dangerous storm that hit Florida's coast. When it did, many negative things occurred such as the destruction of transportation passages and roads, and some lives were taken. The impacts that occurred from this storm will take a long time to repair. This is part of Florida's monthly drill and they know what to do. Bad things will happen to humans only if they don't follow protocols or something goes wrong.

Trip to Tanzania

Over winter break in December 2022, I had the opportunity to go to Tanzania to help the Maasai tribe with their water crisis. We went there under the guidance of the Karimu organization, which went the previous year and built one 100,000-liter water tank for the community. In 2022, a group of five students and I went on a mission to gather data. We wanted to understand how the unit has been utilized so far, and if and how it has changed their lives. We also wanted to deploy weather station units that measure the purity and temperature of the rainwater as well as the wind direction. Recapping the trip, I learned multiple things regarding the Maasai free time, the patriarchy currently in place, and new ways to improve the water crisis.

At the community center where the tank is, I was able to interview some of the Maasai people. After putting all my data together, I learned that the most significant impact of the water tank was the number of kids able to go to school. The water unit enabled double the amount of kids to enroll in the schools. The kids are normally in charge of walking to the dams to get water during the daytime, leaving no time to go to school. However, since the tank is now closer to their *bomas* (small huts made out of cow dung that the Maasai call their homes), kids can get water in less time and make it to school. Not only are the kids able to finally enroll in school, but also the frequency at which they went to school increased significantly as well. The frequency of the students increased by around 150% due to the water tank being closer to the bomas. According to some of the teachers, the students showed up to school with water bottles, and the students were cleaner than before. The students' easier access to water is not only helping their education but their appearance as well.

The water unit that was deployed was not convenient for all. Some whose bomas were further from the community center would still only get water from the dams, despite the water being cleaner in the tank. While the community center tank is meant to help provide cleaner water and save time, it was not the most convenient for some. On the contrary, every single Maasai who lived close to the community center stopped going to dams permanently and went to the tank instead. The Maasai would have to pass the community center to get to dams so not only was the tank water cleaner, but it also saved more than six hours. In the middle of the extremes was the majority–those Maasai who would go to the tanks but also the dams because they were slightly closer to dams or it was more convenient. Overall, the water harvesting unit provided the Maasai with a cleaner, more convenient source of water that also allowed more students to go to school.

Unlike most of the world, the Maasai community revolves around patriarchy. The men are in charge of everyone, and every set of bomas has one male leader. The men's job is to find new wives, take care of the cattle, and sit down. The women's jobs were to walk multiple miles to find water, take care of the kids, build houses, make food for the family, and reproduce. The children's jobs were to learn how to take care of the cattle, learn how to get the water, and if one was the older child, take care of the younger children. The men would have around 15 wives and 40 children, which would create a community. The mothers would then create bomas out of cow dung for their babies and once around 15 are made, the community was complete. The father then spends one night in each boma and rotates continuously. The mothers also go and sell jewelry, and the income is used by the father for whatever he sees fit. In general, money was not a huge problem for the Maasai; the men choose to buy a lot of cattle with the money as they were a form of currency themselves. Overall, it seems gentrification has some effect on the Maasai community. The community wants to improve their lives based on what they see in more modern societies, such as access to water and health. Yet, in some ways, the patriarchal society continues to dominate their way of life.

On the last day of the trip, my colleagues and I collaborated with the leaders and future leaders of the Maasai tribe to brainstorm some ideas for ways to bring water to all of the bomas. We started with some calculations. We figured out that there are 100,000 total Maasai people, 50,000 of whom are a part of the water crisis. We then divided 50,000 by 10 because there are around 10 people per boma. That leaves us with the number 5,000; we had to solve for 5,000 bomas.

We all split into groups of four and came up with at least three solutions. My group's first solution was to create tanks that can hold 20,000 liters, which would be put at all the Maasai centers that have access to the highway. They should have access to the highway because during the dry season, the water tankers can come and refill the tanks. During the rainy season, the rainwater is enough to fill the tanks, so the Maasai will be okay. However, there was a problem. Some of the bomas are very far from the nearest community center. So we created a supplementary solution. We said that we could create dams that have pipes going straight into a 10,000 liter tank near all the bomas that are one hour or longer walk. A second solution was the same as the first plan, except that the truckers would be private because then the Maasai can get water at the exact time they want it.

While we created some concrete ideas, we also had some rough ideas. One was involving drones that can carry 100mL of water at a time and will slowly refill the tanks. The second, which was kind of goofy, involved recreating the tech that Dubai used to create artificial rain clouds. Third was portable water buckets that have a flap that could be opened whenever it rains. The main problem when brainstorming was the cost of the plans. The Maasai who helped make all of this possible (Mbayani Tayai) is also the director of a non-profit organization named Vijana. Between the money within his organization and the $24,088 my friends and I fundraised, we hopefully will have enough to help the water crisis even more.

As I was interviewing the Maasai, when I asked what we could improve I heard a lot of responses regarding having more tanks in general (increase in quantity). Along with that idea, I heard that the tanks should also be more distributed so more bomas can access the water and save more of their valuable time. I also heard that the water tanks should also be put near the schools, or even at the schools because then when students go to school, they can also get water on the way home. Lastly, I heard one extremely unique idea. A teacher wanted me to create a way that makes the tank at the community center operational not only when there is electricity. The tank at the community center only works if there is electricity because there is a filtration system that only works when the power switch is turned on or there is enough solar energy to work.

Overall, I learned a lot on this trip and cannot wait to return back next year with refined ideas on how to bring water to the Maasai.

An Urgent Call to Entomologists

On Friday, October 23, 2019, entomologists in the state of Washington discovered the first nest of murder hornets in the U.S.. This sounds terrifying, mostly because a murder hornet sting is extremely painful and will cause a human arm to swell up like a balloon. I made the mistake of watching a Coyote Peterson video in which he allows himself to be stung by one of these hornets, and it was harder to watch than any horror movie. It's apparently a searing, burning, electric pain that lasts for several minutes. At one point, Peterson had to take off his watch because the swelling in his arm was cutting off circulation to his hand.

As scary as a murder hornet sting sounds, the real threat they pose is to honeybees. They are a ravenous species, and they routinely attack beehives to dig out food. With their strong mandibles, they are able to destroy a honeybee hive in a matter of hours. Why does this matter so much? Since bees pollinate flowers and many food crops, they are central to keep most of nature alive. The U.S. honeybee population is already very low, and with predators like the murder hornet on the scene, the situation will likely get much worse. Put briefly, we need bees, and the murder hornets kill bees. For this reason, the appearance of a murder hornet nest in Washington is a matter of serious concern to us all.

What are murder hornets, exactly? Murder hornets (*vespa mandarinia*) are native to East Asia, and they can grow to be two inches in length. To put this in perspective, common hornets usually measure about one inch in length, and common wasps do not tend to grow past one-half an inch. They make their nests in the ground, and hikers in rural Japan and China can at times be surprised by them and receive painful stings that can in some cases be fatal. Each year, roughly fifty people in Japan die from murder hornet attacks. Even so, murder hornets, which the Japanese refer to as "giant sparrow wasps" (because of their size), have become a kind of delicacy in Tokyo and other Japanese cities. Some restaurants fry the hornet grubs until all the venom is out and mix it with rice. Others deep-fry the hornets and eat them as a snack. Some restaurants even sell liquor made from the hornets, and the venom supposedly gives the liquor a nice kick.

If murder hornets pose such a serious threat to honeybees in the U.S., why aren't they a major threat in Asia? The answer has to do with natural selection. Murder hornets are not a major threat to Asian honeybees because these bees have evolved with effective measures to defend themselves from murder hornets. In short, they lure a scout hornet into their hive and then smother it. Honeybees in the U.S. have not evolved alongside murder hornets, so they do not know how to defend themselves. They treat murder hornets like any other threat, and they die in the thousands when just a handful of these hornets attack the hive. Given this, a small number of murder hornet nests can take out thousands of American beehives.

The swift action of entomologists in Washington saved the region from a wider problem with murder hornets. That said, the problem is far from over. As long as products continue to be shipped back and forth between the U.S. and Asia, there is a chance that animal stowaways like the murder hornet will make their way across the Pacific. There is no easy solution to the threat that the giant Asian hornet poses to American honey bees (and people), but it will be necessary to remain vigilant and support the work of entomologists.

Burma is on Fire

The collapse of democracy in Myanmar is a crisis for democracy everywhere. In the U.S., we witnessed a violent coup attempt on January 6, 2021, but it was thankfully unsuccessful. In Myanmar, which has a long history of colonial and autocratic rule, military officers have successfully replaced a democratically elected government. There are now peaceful pro-democracy protests taking place all over the country, but the military is working to end these, even if it means killing protestors. The potential return to autocratic rule in Myanmar is a real possibility, and this creates a humanitarian, institutional, and strategic problem for the world.

On November 8, 2020, Myanmar held general elections. The results of the election placed the National League of Democracy (NLD), Myanmar's ruling party, back in power. For the majority of Myanmar's history as an independent nation, it has been ruled either by a totalitarian regime or by a military junta. The 2020 elections were only the third round of democratic elections in the country's history, after the fall of the previous military regime in 1990. The hero of the democracy movement, Aung San Suu Kyi, was re-elected as prime minister, and she was ready to be sworn into office on February 2, 2021.

On February 1, 2020, the country's military leaders declared the election results to be illegitimate and took power. They arrested Suu Kyi and other members of the NLD and declared a one-year state of emergency. According to the Carter Center, which observed the election, there were pre-election issues, but "election day itself occurred without major irregularities being reported by mission observers." Nonetheless, the military claimed widespread voter fraud and has held onto power. They have issued statewide media blackouts, arrested numerous people, and co-opted opposition politicians with the promise of influence within the new military regime.

On February 15, 2021, mass protests erupted throughout Myanmar. These had been peaceful protests, but the military responded with lethal force. Over 500 protesters were arrested and over 20 were killed. Subsequently, the armed forces attacked peaceful demonstrators in multiple cities with live ammunition, leaving 18 dead and at least 30 wounded. Since the start of the demonstrations, the armed forces also regularly used tear gas, flash-bang grenades, and stun grenades. A year later, the military has gained control over Burma and is now in power once again.

On March 3, 2021, the protests continued. The army's violent crackdown on the protestors only grew, and many more people died as a result. The question now was whether the UN would get involved to protect Myanmar's election results or at least stop the killing. Since Myanmar is a sovereign nation and the violence hasn't spilled over their borders, the UN may not get involved at all. This places democracy in a dangerous position in Myanmar, and weakens it around the world.

The Year of the Ox

Long ago, the Jade Emperor set out to name the constellations of the zodiac. He decided to hold a contest and name the constellations after the animals that showed up at his palace. The first animal to answer the call was the ox. Enjoying a huge head start, the good-natured ox met a rat along the way. "Can I have a ride?" asked the rat. The ox, not suspecting any chicanery, gladly said yes. When the pair arrived at the palace, the rat leapt off the ox's head and scurried into the palace, effectively arriving first. This is why the rat is the first constellation in the Chinese zodiac and the ox is relegated to second place.

2021 was the Chinese Year of the Ox , and it came on the heels of 2020, which was suitably the year of the rat. What can we expect from the ox? Oxen are industrious, cautious, and generally helpful, so all signs seem positive. The last time it was the year of the ox was 2009. What happened that year? Barack Obama took office as the 44th U.S. president, the Sri Lankan civil war ended, swine flu became a global pandemic, and *Avatar* was released in theaters. In other words, a mixed bag. Before 2009, the last year of the ox was 1997. Malala Yousafzai and Naomi Osaka were both born that year, so maybe there's good cause for hope. What could we expect from 2021? Hopefully, the ox will stay true to character and help us out of our current troubles.

Overall, the year was pretty hectic, the pandemic problems increased and Trump's presidency exit and the new election caused multiple political problems. The Jan 6th problems still carried throughout the year and impacted the years following it as well.

TECHNOLOGY, SCHOOL, AND PANDEMIC

A Transformative Time in History

The Case Against Digital Restrictions

It is increasingly common for young people to spend a lot of time on their smartphones or other digital devices. This has caused many parents to worry that their kids are becoming addicted to social media and losing important life skills. The news that many Silicon Valley execs don't let their kids have social media just reinforces this idea. To cope with this challenge, parents often put time limits and other restrictions on their kids' devices. This is a bad idea.

It's important that young people spend only a reasonable amount of time online. But how do we meet this goal? Putting digital restrictions on kids' phones and tablets only creates an atmosphere of mistrust, surveillance, and top-down authoritarianism. There are digital restrictions in North Korea, Iran, and China as well. Is this the model our parents wish to follow? A better way would be to approach the issue democratically. There can be mutually agreed-upon limits and reasonable penalties for non-compliance. This teaches kids how to make laws, live with them, and face the consequences of not following them. It means more work for parents, but putting in place digital restrictions teaches kids nothing and prepares them only for life in a totalitarian regime.

Is There Such a Thing as Bad Technology?

"Bad workers always blame their tools." The first time I heard this proverb it immediately made me think of the debates currently raging around digital technology. In an article published in the *MIT Technology Review*, for example, we're told, "Screen time might be physically changing kids' brains," and that none of these changes are good. The point seems to be that exposure to tech is bad for our brains, and the blame for this damage lies squarely with the tech itself. But what is our responsibility? Are we right to blame our tools?

The question of whether technology is bad or good largely misses the point. Like all tools, context matters. If I use a bicycle to ride to school, this is good. If I use a bicycle to ride into a pedestrian, this is bad. Is any of this the bike's fault? The same can be said about drugs. If a doctor prescribes a painkiller and it's taken according to the doctor's instructions, then there's no problem. However, if someone buys that same painkiller on the street or takes too much of it, then there can be serious problems. A life-saving medical device in the hands of someone not trained to use it is, by the same logic, a weapon.

It may seem that arguing for the moral neutrality of technology is a pointless exercise. I get this, but it also has important consequences for how we live in the world. By blaming tech, we essentially evade our own responsibility to act ethically and appropriately in the world. The morality of technology, whether by this we mean simple devices like pencils or complex ones like AI, resides with us. How we use technology is who we are. As we work and live in the world, pointing at the evils of technology allows us to feel blameless, even as we do serious (and often unstudied) damage to ourselves and the world around us. "It's not us, it's our tools!" we say, as if to turn our backs on the root of the problem.

What's to be done? The clearest option is probably education. We can have sessions and even classes in school that deal with the moral and neurological impact of digital technology, but we can also invest in humanities courses that help us to think critically and make tough decisions when the correct answer isn't clear. Many kids use fake birth dates to get Apple IDs and Google accounts before they're thirteen. Is this okay? Probably not, but why is it not okay? There's no rulebook for this, and context matters.

In the end, technology is neither bad nor good. It is for us to decide how to use the tools we create and take responsibility for our use. It is worth remembering that in regulating technology, we're really regulating ourselves.

How Sports Rock My Life

Sports have positively impacted my life in three key ways. Mentally, it is a great tool to drive clarity and focus. Socially, it helps encourage team building skills and build social interactions. And physically, it has always helped me keep fit. Many people have always enjoyed sports, and I wonder if people realize how many important benefits that sports can bring to life.

First, mentally, we all have times when we need to think clearly and find focus. When you take breaks, it is good to go outside and play sports. It clears your head and keeps you in good mental shape. According to Peggy Plencher in the 2016 article, "The Top 7 Mental Benefits of Sports,"

> Whether you are playing sports, working out at a gym, or taking a brisk walk, physical activity triggers brain chemicals, endorphins, that make you feel happier and more relaxed. Team sports in particular provide a chance to unwind and engage in a satisfying challenge....

These facts seek to explain how playing sports can make your brain think differently, access varied perspectives, and solve a problem in creative ways. This is significant because it helps your problem-solving abilities tremendously. Endorphins are chemicals that produce happiness in your brain, which can help with focus. When I am stuck on a problem, I play a sport as a break and it helps me look at the solution differently. In conclusion, sports have helped me look at problems in many ways and have helped me restore my tank when I'm in need of stamina.

Second, sports assist in communicating with others and with team skills. This is because in order to play well, you need to talk with others on your team. Individuals can make friends in the process, who always will have something new to teach you. Sports helps me make friends and clear my head. For example, I am on a soccer team, and I make many friends playing the sport. Another example of how sports is helpful to building communication is the focus and attention it requires. When I am in a soccer game, I have to pay attention to the game and help my team by communicating. These skills can help in other settings, from raising your hand in class all the way to conducting a job interview. Communication helps tremendously and is a really important skill to learn. In conclusion, sports can help your communication skills and team building skills.

Lastly, sports keep you in good shape. Ironically, when we were in the middle of a global crisis, the Covid-19 pandemic, we had to practice social distancing. You can complete your work while staying inside, but you also have the opportunity to get exercise and it will help you stay in shape. For example, I was eating a lot during quarantine but I also played lots of sports to keep me in shape. Sports helped me stay in shape and I am still in good shape and plan on staying that way! Why am I still doing sports? Well, I am doing sports because it feels right to stay in shape and stay healthy otherwise I'm going to have bigger problems in life. Without sports I would probably not be as in good shape. Once, I had an ankle injury that lasted three months and prevented me from playing sports. During that time I realized how essential sports can be to my life and how difficult it was to operate without such activity.

In the end, sports are good for you for many reasons and these were just a few of them. Sports can help you have fun and can help you socially as well. Physical and mental state is important, and sports can help you to balance both. Sports are essential to doing well in life and for your health. Sports have rocked my life!

Sophomore W Period

The school I attended created a new period called the "W" period. W period is a time where students at Sacred Heart Prep (SHP) get to have valuable community-life time as well as occasionally have an extra class led by entire departments. According to Ms. Lauren Benjamin, assistant principal for Mission and Culture, the main goal of W period is "for dedicating time to discuss topics that are not able to be discussed in the classroom … and to dedicate face-to-face time for teachers and students to work on things that would normally be a Schoology post." This offers time for classmates and teachers to connect beyond the academic side. This way students can reflect on themselves, their relationships, and their personalities in a more personal connection and intimate space. Ms. B. also acknowledged that "[she] understands that students have things that they are going through and won't always like W period." But she says that constructive feedback will help improve the period so everyone will enjoy it as well as teach the topics for students' needs.

Furthermore, she says, it offers a space for the "stuff that is already identified as a need… but we haven't had enough space because we prioritize academic classes." One of Sacred Heart's goals for educating students is to improve the whole student. While academics are the most important piece of our education, we also have to acknowledge the personal growth and reflection piece that the W period accomplishes and works towards improving. W period is also "framed around the question 'what does it mean to be a Sacred Heart student?'"

An example of face-to-face interaction during the W period is service learning. While the W period might not be the most academic time, it does teach students about social lessons, health, and awareness. However, the W period can be used by academic departments as well. For example, in one W period, because the sophomore class was reading Frederick Douglass's account of his experience of enslavement, the sophomore English team led a W period featuring episode 3 of the acclaimed Netflix series, "High on the Hog," which examines the influence of enslaved people on the food that we eat today, and which has largely been ignored for years. The period also included reflection on family food traditions and journaling.

According to one student, "instead of W period, students can spend time with teachers and have extra office hours during the day, so then we can all be better in our studies." While W period is a new addition to the schedule, and there are pros, the majority of students I interviewed preferred another gator block (an extra period at SHP where students can join clubs, go to teachers, or simply study) to seize other opportunities.

Another student said, "While I do like the idea of W period, I think the space could be used much more efficiently to best benefit SHP students." She believed that community life and appreciating each other are important, but also thinks that this time during the day is valuable and can be used for students to excel in academics. She also suggested that in order to improve the W periods, she "would love to see more activities that benefit students in ways other than sit-down presentations" and also wants to "see ways in which students can relate to things." A lot of the presentations are teachers trying to teach typical important principles. But new things that students have not learned such as improving collaboration skills, developing empathic approaches, improving listening skills, and improving the ability to learn from others, might be a new way for educators to approach W period.

Lastly, I spoke to a third student who did not enjoy the W period. He said, "It is not helpful whatsoever. I can't recall a time when I have come out of the W period having learned something valuable about our community. It is a time that could be much better used for students to catch up on work or study for a test." He believes that the W period was an unnecessary addition to the schedule, and that community life gatherings explore the main points of the W period.

Overall, the W period was originally a good idea, but after a couple of months, it was proven to be a time that could be better used doing other activities. Ultimately, the W period changed a little as it has not been adjusted to being an extended lesson from the academic departments. Students' opinions were able to help the office understand what students think of the period and let the office know exactly how to fix it.

New Academic Policies and Student Learning

The Sacred Heart Preparatory (SHP) administration established new academic policies for the 2022-2023 school year. The new policies included stricter enforcement of tardies, longer passing periods, a new homework policy, and changes to policies surrounding academic integrity. With over two months of school already gone, the policy changes went into effect. We sat down with Mr. Jorge Reyes, assistant principal of curriculum, Dr. Jennie Whitcomb, SHP principal, and Dr. Diana Neebe, assistant principal of instruction & faculty development, to talk about these changes and how they came to be.

Mr. Reyes announced, "There are only three main changes: the tardy policy, the longer passing periods, and the new homework policy." He explained that the policies are meant to guide students. There were some other minor changes as well. For example, students can no longer get an "incomplete course." Furthermore, Mr. Reyes explained the new attendance policy requires that "if a student is absent for more than 20% of classes, then the student has to petition for credit."

The SHP community believes that being in class is important for the student and for their classmates as well. Mr. Reyes described the homework policy as: "if a student is missing an assessment or three assignments in one class, then the student is required to attend the homework center." The rationale behind this is that if a student is missing three assignments, that means that they have not paid attention or participated in class for a whole week. Lastly, according to Mr. Reyes, the longer passing period was set in place because "it allows students to get to class on time and get a break." Students now receive a longer, more manageable break between classes, meaning that theoretically, they have no reason to be late.

Dr. Whitcomb explained that the most effective policy so far from the school's perspective is "the tardy policy, but it is hard to know if it is the policy itself or the enforcing of the policy." This means that there is no definitive "most effective" policy; rather, all the policies are effective only if the students follow them. However, she viewed the tardy policy "as a win because students are starting to feel the need to get to class on time more often." She also related this to the extension of five-minute passing periods to ten-minute passing periods when she said, "Students are starting to stop trickling in for the first twenty minutes of class" and were now instead "showing up on time."

With students coming in on time, the teachers are able to make every seventy-five minutes of a class count. She also said that the ten-minute passing periods "can provide a break to students who are having a tough day, can allow students to go to the bathroom, and can allow students to have more time to get to classes." The extension of passing periods seems to be an effective policy, allowing teachers and students to take advantage of the full seventy-five minute periods.

Dr. Whitcomb said she could not judge the incomplete course policy because "it is too early because it is at a semester level." Dr. Whitcomb believed that it was also "too early" to determine whether the homework policy is effective or not because it was only a month into school. She strongly emphasized that the "homework policy is there to guide students towards learning... and following the policy will ultimately result in the student's success." The policy was involved because it helps students follow the Sacred Heart goals as well as thrive in their classes. Overall, Dr. Whitcomb believed that each of the new rules were set in place to help students follow and benefit from the SHP goals.

In addition to the tardy policy, SHP took a novel approach to academic discipline and integrity, according to Dr. Neebe. Dr. Neebe said the main group that signed off on these policies was the COR Leadership team, which includes the principal, assistant principal, director of Counseling & Advising, and the head of OMCS. The COR group that signed off on these policies was a diverse one, incorporating multiple departments. After an infraction of the academic integrity policy, Dr. Neebe said, "Typically a teacher's first person to report to is their department chair." She said that one of the biggest changes made was to make the first step of reporting to the department chair and then consulting with Mr. Reyes, head of academics at SHP.

The goal of the new changes was to ensure that department chairs are notified of the infractions and are consulted in the process. Dr. Neebe added, "Depending on what the nature of the infraction is, it goes to Mr. Quattlebaum, assistant principal of Sacred Heart Preparatory." She emphasizes the importance of separating disciplinary action from the student's learning process. Moreover, she added that the students' learning remains a priority and that the process for an infraction of the academic integrity policy will remain a separate issue. The main goal of the policy changes was "to help dissuade students from making poor choices," Dr. Neebe said. The new policy changes also hold students accountable for their actions and doing the learning. Dr. Neebe states that the reason students do not get an automatic zero is that "we want to make sure you're held to the task of doing the learning." For example, if a student were to cheat on a quiz, they would be retaking it instead of just getting an automatic zero. However, there is a grade penalty for cheating, meaning that students are given a second chance to demonstrate their knowledge but an academic penalty is given. Students must put in the hard work of learning and "cheating won't be an easy out." The school has been working diligently to prevent cheating and has used W period as a way to work with the 9th and 10th grades about the importance of academic integrity. The policy changes were designed to not hinder students' learning and keep the disciplinary action separate.

Aside from faculty, the students at SHP share a wide variety of opinions regarding the new policy changes. One senior thought that new "absences and homework policies [are] a good reminder to students that we have a good education [and] help instill new habits." He found that the stricter tardy and homework policies prevented students from submitting late assignments and being late to classes, unlike in years prior. Furthermore, he believed the extended passing periods are a good thing because they "give students a way to transition between topics in class [and]…you don't have to try sprinting to your next class." Although he agreed with the ten-minute passing periods, he expressed his dissatisfaction with the short lunch period as well as a five-minute passing period after lunch instead of a ten-minute passing period. He viewed the new policy changes as beneficial to the school as a whole.

A freshman explained that having a strict tardy policy was extremely important and "time and learning at this school is super valuable." He believed that enforcing a stricter tardy policy keeps students engaged and ready for class, and does not waste precious class time. He claimed that having ten-minute passing periods is beneficial to students' learning because they are not given any other breaks besides lunch throughout the day. Finally, when informed of the new retake policy that pertains to instances of academic dishonesty, he believed that it was a good thing that students would not receive an automatic zero. Although there is a penalty, he believed that giving a student a zero does not "reflect their understanding and comprehension of the material" and giving them a chance to retake "is valuable to show what they have been learning in the class."

Omicron Infection

As the new year of 2022 was approaching, public health experts warned and expected that the new Omicron variant of Covid-19 would produce a steep rise in infections and hospitalizations shortly after the new year. In the face of this grim news, many people wondered how this variant emerged and how contagious it really was. There was also a good deal of concern about vaccinations and where we stand with prevention and other treatments. The Omicron variant presented a large number of challenges, but these can be met with the proper information and resources. This dependence on information was true at the start of the pandemic and has not changed since.

Scientists first detected the Omicron variant in South Africa. By late November of 2021, it had become a "variant of concern." There are three possible theories regarding its origin. The first is that it developed in immuno-compromised patients in a South African hospital. The second theory is that it emerged through reverse zoonosis—by humans infecting an animal with Covid-19 and the virus mutated when passed back to humans. The third theory is that it emerged as a response to the antiviral drug Molnupiravir, which hospitals in South Africa commonly use to combat Covid infections. Whatever the case, we know that the Omicron variant has over 50 novel mutations on its spike protein compared to the original Wuhan virus.

All these mutations mean that the Omicron variant spreads three times more easily than the Delta variant. The CDC has warned that someone infected with the Omicron variant can easily spread the virus to others, even if they are vaccinated or are asymptomatic. Carl Zimmer and Andrew Jacobs, writing for the *New York Times*, reported that there is no real consensus about why Omicron spreads so easily. "One possibility," they claim, "is that it can invade cells more readily; other possibilities include an ability to multiply once inside cells." Whichever of these possibilities is true, it seems logical to focus our resources on prevention rather than treatments. However, while prevention is important, resources should also be spent towards vaccines. Vaccines are important and the only reason why South Africa is suffering is because of the lack of doses they receive. This is a great example of why the inequity in global healthcare affects everyone, not just the citizens within underserved countries.

In terms of prevention, a combination of vaccine booster shots, face masks, and rapid home tests have been and still are the best line of defense. Studies showed that a third Pfizer shot, for example, provides the same level of protection as two shots against the original strain of Covid-19. In a sense, it will be necessary to change what society means by "vaccinated" in the U.S.; this meant two shots in early 2021, but by December 2021, it meant three. Face masks are also effective to slow the spread of the Omicron variant, since infection still requires exposure to the sort of droplets that enter the air when we speak or sneeze. Another useful tool is the rapid home test, which checks for Covid antigens and produces results in about fifteen minutes. Maskless gatherings indoors should take place only after participants get a negative test result. They should also be vaccinated and have had three Pfizer shots. These may seem like serious inconveniences, but preventing the spread of the Omicron variant is essential for the safety of the world.

All things considered, everyone needs to be more careful despite the presence of effective vaccines. Those who are not vaccinated need to get vaccinated. This way, they only have to worry about one variant and not all the others. Those who are unvaccinated can also inadvertently make new variants. As with many things, prevention is the key. While time has passed, the lesson has not changed. We are all in this together.

Covid-19 and Middle School

One thing we figured out over the first six months of our Covid experience in 2020 is that online learning is exhausting. Beyond the fact that we were stuck at home, we were forced to spend most of our day sitting in the same chair, staring at the same small screen. We wrestled with buggy online software and tried our best to get through written instructions, all while never going off camera or eating any snacks. It started to feel like a punishment after a while. To add to the pain, we couldn't see our friends and unwind between classes or after school. When you add to this the fact that many of us deal with distractions at home and even unreliable internet connections, it's a wonder we were able to learn anything at all. Our teachers helped a lot, but then there's only so much anyone can do.

First things first: Zoom fatigue is real. As it turns out, humans evolved talking to one another mostly in person. Now a lot of what we do when we talk face-to-face is handled unconsciously through body language, leaving our conscious brains to handle just some of the information. As Libby Sander and Oliver Bauman[12] explain, "Meeting online increases our cognitive load, because several of its features take up a lot of conscious capacity." Without body language, our conscious mind has to figure out a lot more about what's going on. Is the other person serious or joking? Are they being ironic or sincere? Our brains have to work harder to figure all this

---

[12] Sander, Libby, and Oliver Bauman. "Zoom Fatigue is Real— Here's Why Video Calls Are So Draining." Ted, 19 May 2020, ideas.ted.com/zoom-fatigue-is-real-heres-why-video-calls- are-so-draining/

out online, especially when the audio and video are cutting out.

Since early March of 2019, it was also nearly impossible to see my friends. I remember how it used to be: seeing friends in the hall between classes, joking around at lunch, hanging out after school and playing sports on the weekends. It all feels like it was years ago. We had online hangouts, but they're lame. Even multiplayer video games lost some of their appeal. Before the pandemic, I was allowed to run around outside for about two hours a day. My mom saw it as healthy exercise and part of my development, but I was just happy to play sports for 120 minutes a day. Since that March, the run-wild time vanished, only to resume in 2022. Instead, I spent my day pretty much either in class or studying, with only short breaks for socially distanced outdoor activities. After spending a long day in front of a screen, a middle schooler just needs more running around.

Online schooling also opens up the thorny issue of distractions. Not everyone has siblings or pets at home, but there are always things to take your focus away from schoolwork. Even if we think reading ten pages on gravity is interesting, it's hard to pay attention when the dog is barking, trucks are picking up the trash, leaf blowers are roaring, and parents are in the next room talking on the phone. I have a reasonably quiet place to work, but some students work in common areas at home, where there's even more noise and lots of distractions. It's one thing to do your homework at the kitchen table, but it's another to try and attend all your classes at that table. And this all assumes that there's no problem with the internet connection (though of course there are always problems).

When we thought there was no end in sight for the pandemic, we needed to make the best of online schooling. Just in case something like this happens again, here are some suggestions: More time in breakout rooms, and maybe allowing some private chatting would likely help. It's hard to sit in front of a screen for hours and never ask your friends questions or even crack jokes, after all. Converting some of the lessons to short audio podcasts and limiting homework would also help get us away from our laptops. These are small improvements, but they could go a long way toward helping us survive what was left of the strangest school year of our lives (so far), and any other years that will show their nasty head in the future.

What We've Lost, What We'll (Hopefully) Gain

It's amazing how much I took for granted. I played sports, my family traveled, my grandparents visited, I went to school, and the internet had entertaining stories on all sorts of things. All of that disappeared when the pandemic began. The Covid-19 pandemic was a struggle for teenagers in many ways, but the main source of our pain was the loss of social networks and all the contact with friends and family that made our world livable. The only thing that made it bearable was knowing that we were saving lives and that it wouldn't last forever. Sometimes I wondered, though, what will come out of this. What will the new normal look like?

Social networks—friends, extended family, and classmates—make up most of a teenager's life. As psychology professor Catherine Bagwell points out, "Adolescence is a time when forming and maintaining close, intimate friendships is a critical developmental task —a main 'job' of being an adolescent."[13] She goes on to say that much of this work happens in "face-to-face interactions when teens gather in the basement, legs and arms entwined as three or four pile on a couch talking and hanging out, or at the school lunch table when a dozen teens sit together at a table designed for half as many." All of this closeness is important for our development and happiness. It's one thing to play virtual tennis online with a friend, but it's a whole other thing to

---

[13] Bagwell, Catherine. "Teens are Wired to Resent Being Stuck with Parents and Cut Off from Friends During Coronavirus Lockdown." The Conversation, 22 Apr. 2020, theconversation.com/teens-are-wired-to-resent-being-stuck-with-parents-and-cut-off-from-friends-during-coronavirus-lockdown-136435

be playing actual sports with friends. Social distancing took this away, and we didn't get it back until 2022.

There is some comfort in knowing that our pain is saving lives. The city of San Francisco government website put it clearly: "Stay Home. Save Lives." In an April 15, 2020 article for WTTV Chicago, Heather Cherone reports that according to city data, Chicago's stay-at-home order has "saved nearly 1,700 lives"[14] in that city. These are dramatic numbers, and they show that social distancing slowed down the infection rate and kept people alive. My mom's parents live in Ohio, and they are both in their 80s. When I got bored or frustrated at home, I thought of them and I hoped that young people in their state were also doing the right thing to keep my family safe. Maybe there are kids in Ohio with grandparents in Menlo Park, so I was helping to keep their family safe while they were doing what they could to protect mine.

All this talk about protecting the vulnerable makes me think about how ideas of community and social networks might change after the pandemic ends. Will I feel closer to those kids in Ohio who stayed in and saved my grandparents? Will they feel grateful to us for protecting their grandparents? Will this bring us together? Are there other ways that this pandemic can help us to be connected? Most of the news I read is pretty negative, but there are signs of hope. In Albany, NY, for example, there was a boom in community gardening that is "helping to save money and [...] getting people outside during the

---

14 Cherone, Heather. "Stay-at-Home Order Saved Nearly 1,700 Lives in Chicago: City Data." WTTV, 15 Apr. 2020, news.wttw.com/ 2020/04/15/stay-home-order-saved-nearly- 1700-lives-chicago-city-data

Covid-19 pandemic."[15] It's also a positive step forward in the fight against climate change. Even in the Middle East, there was talk of hope. In Israel, the national healthcare system was bringing Jews, Muslims, and Christians together in a unified effort to halt the spread of the virus. As Yossi Klein Halevi reported, Israel was now in a position to turn "crisis into opportunity" and build a unified society that is secure and free.[16]

In the end, there was no way to spin this pandemic into a good thing. It just wasn't. The United States has 4% of the world's population, but we had over a third of the world's coronavirus infections. Over thirty-million Americans went without work, and over one million have died so far. Despite the bad news, there is reason to believe that the shelter-in-place order saved lives and that new possibilities came out of this hardship. I am happy that I was there to help make that happen.

---

[15] Finley, Louis. "Community Gardens Bringing People Together During Pandemic." News 10, 28 Apr. 2020, www.news10.com/news/local-news/community-gardens-bringing- people-together-during-pandemic/

[16] Halevi, Yossi Klein. "Israel's Arab Moment: In This Pandemic, The Nation's Citizens Face a Crisis that is Finally Bringing us Together." The Atlantic, 30 Apr. 2020, www.theatlantic.com/ideas/archive/2020/04/israels-arab-moment/610918/

Arhaan Gupta-Rastogi

I am currently a junior in high school studying a wide range of topics with a focus on computer science and the natural sciences. I believe that empowering each person with their voice is one of the most democratic rights we have. At school, I am learning the many topics and skills required to solve the global challenges we face.

Over the years, I have taken the time to note my thoughts, whether online on my blog, in school with our newspaper, or in my community with my opinion editorials in regional publications. I enjoy understanding current events, establishing a point of view, sharing my opinions, and hearing from and conversing with everyone. We have lived through some of the most amazing and yet challenging times from the pandemic to elections to technological changes and our generation's perspective is important to capture.

Outside of school, I am a researcher at the Martinos Center for Biomedical Imaging at Harvard University doing computational data analysis. There is so much potential to improve treatment outcomes and patient care with technology, and I want to apply my skills to those problems. I co-authored a scholarly paper on the history of blood transfusions as a research intern at Stanford University. Within my school and community, I serve as managing editor of digital channels for my school's newspaper, sit on U.S. Representative Anna Eshoo's Student Advisory Board, teach myself computer languages, and play varsity tennis.

www.ingramcontent.com/pod-product-compliance
Lightning Source LLC
Chambersburg PA
CBHW052119030426
42335CB00025B/3062